PITCH

LAKE

ANDRE BAGOO

PITCH

LAKE

PEEPAL TREE

First published in Great Britain in 2017
Peepal Tree Press Ltd
17 King's Avenue
Leeds LS6 1QS
UK

ISBN 13: 9781845233532

Supported using public funding by
ARTS COUNCIL
ENGLAND

Now I am a lake

— Sylvia Plath, 'Mirror'

CONTENTS

PITCH

BLACK BOX

LAKE

PITCH

LAKE CHAD

When we walked out the sea had vanished,
when we blinked we saw a lake
but it was dark and we did not know
if we could trust our eyes.

Two thousand deaths they say; none know
they raze our houses, only guns survive;
all schools are emptied for this lesson,
our blood, like the lake, slowly dries.

AFTER ALFRED MENDES, *PITCH LAKE,* 1934

The dirt, the steam, the tar. The path that takes you far from the shop, the smell of a hot kiss – soft, spongy and then unyielding like hardened pitch. The wound, the cut, the oil. The scientists disagree: why is there life where life should not be? The corpse, the bird, the spell. Time a carpet that bells. We break up. Clumps of regret bathe in molasses. Walk on, on the first roads of Washington and New York. The bottle, the rope, the ship. The crenulations of bark, the circles inside a tree, the waves of asphalt, feelers growing like the sea. In these sulphur pools I see the craters of Titan. The indecisive grass is drowned. Under this marbled tarpaulin spirits fight. Mark their rounded mounds, their bubbling cries. The stomach, the whale, the curse. Should I? Could I? What will they think? What do I feel? Will I heal? Will I break? The pit, the pith, the *piche*. Bacteria wed to stone, yearning for home. Go to the door. Open it. Step onto it. The house, the wind, the ache. Remember, nobody sees the same lake.

ON TITIAN'S *DIANA AND ACTAEON*

August. The asphalt
road to Trafalgar Square,
as hot as Trinidad noon.
Like the pigeons, the world flocks,
a legion of specks on the steps of the
National Gallery where they hang
Diana and Actaeon.
Titian's scene could be the Caribbean,
sky as blue as Lear's macaw,
wood that could be rainforest, nude
Diana and her five maids
like a lost Carnival band.
In a corner a black woman stands
outraged, the shadow
of a race's conscience.
Though frozen, she whispers
to all who can see:
Such as I am, you will be,
such as you are, I was –
free. A nation spent millions
on this property but she,
not Actaeon, pays the price.

THE BODY IN THE RIVER

We cannot know her legendary head,
only a torso left, arms, legs – Eve
of Frankenstein's labour. The blue
barrel floats, like baby Moses borne by the
Nile. It carries the empress, naked as paper.
What would Botticelli make of this?
Venus torn into dangling limbs
that silence water, silence air,
pitch roads, silent, kiskadees, silent,
dead museum of forensic trees.
Mitan
mitan
mon coeur
Eden.

We cannot know her legendary head,
crowned now by Sargasso,
sea-eyes that swim to heaps of pearls,
great anchors, wedges of gold.
We cannot know her other shores
where seaweeds make slender patterns,
trails of termites
in the hot house
on the day her destiny becomes clear.
No river is more silent than this.

THE GAOL AT PORT OF SPAIN

And in Eden they build a prison —
chains, pulleys, *cachots brulants*,
the mad jailer's sensual devices
concealed by a montage of stone,
thick walls squaring the world.
They torture a magician here
a slave who tries to disappear.
His body, the chattel, will not yield
to sorcery. More punishment
is applied, justice is done. Yet,
you cannot steal what nobody has made:
property of all is property of none.
For this crime no one pays.

ON WORDSWORTH'S 'THE DAFFODILS'

In Trinidad we don't have daffodils, he said,
And it is wrong to write of foreign things.
But it dawned on me, the poet's sadness,
How only a man pensive and weary
Would prefer flowers to people,
Would retreat, every now and then,
To remember that day on the hill
When even the clouds were lonely.
Isn't that the same country?

KISKADEE

Black like a mind at night
swallowing a canary and
white dove mid-flight
as monogamous as crows
despite a campaign of gun
and dynamite their flock grows
kiskadee kiskadee kiskadee
stealing sugar from kitchen bowls
soul
of echo
no echo now
bodies
vanish among the light poles

SANDRA BLAND CHANGING LANES

a hand
a branch
a swimmer drowning in sand
her hand, as the officer pinned her to the ground
her offence, changing
lanes without signalling
in a cell, she was hanged

did she hear the kiskadees
that sunny afternoon
her heart beating faster
the man telling her to out her cigarette
But I am in my car!

did she realise she'd swim all the way here
to a beach crowded with turtles, crawling
like dinosaurs in Jurassic Park – the hatchlings racing
past corbeaux to the water's edge

> flowing like the river we found at dawn
> we are here to receive her

>> *ouvre baye pou mwen, Ago eh!*
>> *ouvre baye pou mwen,*
>> *ouvre baye pou mwen,*
>> *pou mwen passe.*

POUI

The first night you don't dream.
You come prepared to sleep. You
walk with your pillow, though you forget
your toothbrush and say my books will not do.

You, by the second night, wake screaming.
It's okay, you say, it was just a nightmare.
You had dreamt of flowers upon flowers,
gold petals coating the island like butterflies,
an island so warm tears vanish,
but some of us are blooming
and others not.

Today I watch the pillow you left
on my bed, and try to remember
what I was dreaming that hot night.

KISKADEE

Two weeks later, I woke
I smelled smoke
the kind you cannot see
kiss me, kiskadee
the kind you cannot see
though you know
you can be free
you know
a bush fire is raging
I go flying
the asphalt roads are streams
I watch him each day
like a mirror he answers
two weeks later, I turn
to check, to see
Is he next to me?

SARGASSUM AT MAYARO

They talk of Atlantis
but here is the drowned kingdom:

crabs, shrimp, molluscs clinging
like immigrants to a raft

driftwood through time.
Forget Columbus, this is El Dorado,

invasion of gold berries, honey weeds
that wreathe legs, manacles –

a wave to end all waves,
a nation east of Brazil

warmed by wrongs
until free.

REDHEAD BAY, CUMANA

Even the beach is deceptive
a piece of wood turns into a dolphin
a rock is really soft clay
all things come undone at Redhead Bay
I go, I go, I go, I go –
exploring a mile I'll never know
no beach has an end
I cannot escape you
but the long day must end
in a few hours, the sea takes back everything
the blue rope it snakes ashore
sea-coconuts rolling, like heads, back to sea,
bottles and rubbish that never really disappear
they will disappear
until then, write it in sand
be equal to the pale classes, the other men
surf the hills that are green waves
though nobody hears, nobody sees
what else are we meant to do
if not climb the almond trees?

CONTACTS

Every morning I put them in.
I wake the lenses from their jellied pools
where they spend the night, lids shut.
I feel guilty stirring them,
tiny orphan bubbles, far from any sea,
each as slight as an eyelash.

How strange that such things
can sheath blindness with vision,
make the world as clear as tears.
How vital such membranes must be
to the person who wears them
for the purpose of turning brown green,
letting us see through change.

Every morning I put in my contacts
yet, for years, I cannot see.

ON WALCOTT'S *TI JEAN AND HIS BROTHERS*

The stage on which the actors perform
is comprised of words as solid as limbs,
bodies that move in and out of light
illuminating all of us in the dark stalls. We watch
and are watched by the cast, their starry eyes
trained on our thoughts, the theatre a mind
each member a story, a memory, a grain.
No thought for the child in a black corner
of the room, who shivers because of that word,
a single word which breaks this suspension –
disbelief that anyone could casually throw
such harpoons: faggot, faggot, fag.
When at home that night, the child will read
the dictionary, will learn the different
meanings: a bundle of sticks, a cigarette,
a type of meal, a woman. The child will try to
remember the virtues of Ti Jean, the moral of
the story but wonder: *Is this fable meant for me?*

ERASURE OF HORACE'S EPODE IX,

TRANSLATED FROM THE LATIN BY RON HORNING

When

      shall we praise

             by drinking

     you

   by hearing

         the sea   son

   fled   burning ships

                  chains

            slaves   friends.

Now

    sold   a woman's kiss

        erect

   the shrivelled tits

        ripples   sunlight

  among the dishonoured standards.

Rearing

    chanting   snorting

     the enemy   to the left

We've won already

We've won already

        a salted grave

    purple   soldier

 sails   one hundred   cities

         coast

driven   plunging   rough

   fighting   winds

 break   fill

   flasks

pour the last
  fears   selves
                    wash away.

MONDAY

Sun first
then white sheets
our bodies dropped from our minds
into a bed so warm it breathes,
the weekend's jeans a moult
a denim waterfall crumpled on the floor,
coffee as strong as a ring,
steam as hot as the iron I use
to press my shirt for today's work.

Maybe loving is like ironing a shirt.
Only through heat and pressure does it yield
its shape,
take the form which best fits.
Over time, the cloth's
colours might hold;
or the fabric fade and fray,
the shirt still kept, still worn
but while scrubbing floors, changing
curtains, cutting weeds
slowly grown among
our chive and mint;
or perhaps the shirt is slit for a quilt,
made into a rag,
or given to someone else
who would otherwise be naked.

LOROS GUAROS

I read a bush-fire killed them
these parrots of the Northern Range,
the orange of their wings
bright like eyes staring
at spreading flame,
their cries muffled by mountain,
bodies falling, as Icarus did, back
to darkness, each winged soul
nothing but smoke.

The poui trees remember them.

HERO

They held the funeral at the bar
which made sense: it was a celebration;
when he was alive he would sit out front
on the concrete benches painted forest green.
It made sense, the way death makes sense
of everything, brings each story to a neat ending,
though a life is unending, because a soul is
never born and is therefore ageless, according
to the pundit. They called him Hero,
no doubt because of what he did
on that trip to Carriacou when the boat rocked in stormy sea
and he calmed each passenger; or maybe because of
private acts now made public by tears –
who says big men don't cry?
At funerals we stand for the dead
when the casket comes women cover their heads
sons in white kurtas encircle their father,
sails stirring time, they laurel him
with flowers. Layers and layers of marigolds
and geraniums – for death is beauty, too.
The tallest building in the world must one day crumble,
the pundit says, and the soul lingers for thirteen days.

THE UNDERSEA VOLCANO

Kick'em Jenny might erupt any moment.
Doesn't change a thing for me.
I'll still sneak out of the office quietly,
hoping nobody sees what nobody sees.
I'll borrow six books from the library,
take a Belmont taxi – they seat four or three – pass
the neighbours who don't know my name,
walk up the steps and unlock the padlocked gates
that protect me from everything but me.
My homecoming, an empty apartment
where paintings still line the floor, though
the moving boxes are months gone.
I'll cook a meal to feed the famished day,
talk to the friend who lives in another country,
think of calling my parents, but decline.
I'll recline on my comfortable sofa – where I once
made out with a man who did not love me –
and think of tomorrow, and tomorrow,
and tomorrow. Sleep, my true love, will come
to my bed, I will pull the night around us,
black sheet taut like my eyelids, a starry grave.
Sleep. And the next day, I might wake,
I might once more see the sunlight of eternity
and the unjust world.

THE GYM

These men know
you tear muscle
for it to grow
stronger, bigger,
the heart opening
as far as it can go.

THE HAIRCUT

I don't remember my first haircut
but I remember who did it.
My mother, in those days, was spry
her clippers singing a complicated melody
setting loose frayed edges,
making room for growth, like
cutting grass, like cutting cane, my head
tenderly in her hands, black hair slipping
between fingers. The years.

She can't cut my hair now
and to this man in the noisy salon
my head might as well be a coconut
nothing precious, nothing he hasn't seen,
salt and pepper threads falling to the
tired floor, his blade
a cutlass thrashing.

SHELLS

Here, it reminds me somehow of you.
— Mervyn Taylor, 'The White Shell'

A palm open to nothing.
— Harriet Brown, 'Shell'

I

I found it in the wash, the brown
shell I picked up from the beach
that last day, the little tornado
torn open,   smooth, muscular,
alien among my cottons and whites.
We did not say goodbye. But this relic,
once tossed by rough waves, once
the home of something, houses us.
I wish I had kept more, made
a chorus safe inside my folds,
multitudinous

II

every palm tree has scars

rings on its trunk mark the years

like the lines inside a shell

hard sheaths protect the leaves

though one day each crown must die

for the tree to give life again

III

Mother, in your hands
are the days, gallery rooms
in which you hand the ocean,
or the shock of the blueness of a uniform
on the first day of school when you leave me
standing at the door to the classroom
and say *I am coming back; it will be okay,*
or that day on the bay when the
waves made sand into quicksand
and as I sank I felt I could disappear
into the life that was still to come

IV

together at last
our dreaming eyelids shut
our bodies clammed in fibrous vessels
messages   thoughts
hopes   fears   memories
each whorl a masterpiece, studding
the white walls of our thoughts
Where are we now?

THE BEACH HOUSE

I gave it back to the sea, to dance in.
— George Mackay Brown, 'Beachcomber'

Monday I find a piece of wood
jutting out the sand like a dark tongue
before waves free it, set it adrift –
floating to the part of the ocean
we never see.

Tuesday an old boat washes ashore.
Villagers say it belonged to Mr Brown
who is long dead. No one knows where
he tethered his boat after a long day
casting heavy nets on water.

Wednesday the children find a turtle.
They poke its shell to try to figure
the difference between animal and
rock. A child says the turtle is looking
for someone.

Thursday the house is too hot
so I open all the windows. I look at the deck
where Father would lie in the hammock
like a fish caught in a net, serene,
knowing our destiny.

Friday the dream comes again,
the same path surrounded by hibiscus,
red flowers soft as sea-foam,
and then a choir sings in the night;
the music of a conch shell.

Saturday we pray.
You say faith will let her live longer.
By the third decade of the Rosary I leave.
Walking on the beach alone, the waves
are angry and afraid.

Sunday I wake in the sand.
I forget who I am
and this island, with its perfect coconut trees,
says not to think of heaven.
I find it in the sea.

LOVE

Pitch lake for an eye.
He stares because he knows
even after death hair grows,
ripples in the wind tunnel of time.
He stares because he sees
a school of corbeaux curating the city,
pterodactyls hunting in tar.
These days, dinosaurs fly out the oily depths,
saying time be damned, Earth be damned.
Give us another chance.

BLACK BOX

AFTER OLIVE SENIOR, 'FLYING'

light   smoke   how to dance
disco ball blocked by bodies
the sun eclipsed by moons
men growing like trees
in this club we leap
we do not look
yet look at me now Grandma
whatever I'm drinking it's right
now I don't care what Buju said
or the poet who called me buller
let our republic spread
above clouds – a dance-floor
of dreams
                          leap
like that time at your house Grandma
when walls disappeared
and he called me into the night
called me through the night
all through the gentle night
call, called to light – this sapwood
this heartwood no nails only bone
empty core mystery   bark crackling
there is human flesh in me
                          in forest we
run deep
until trees no longer have meaning
Hurry up. Rain is coming. Let's go.
there is a dance better than geography
he is a poem yet to be danced
Lay with me he says after the club
Grandma I'm not sick
I am love
no one tells you
there is no time without man

there is only bliss
we don't need potions to fly
when we have this

AFTER CHARL LANDVREUGD,
MOVT NR. 8: THE QUALITY OF 21

Dream of rooms, forgetting how to see.
As silent as paintings. Space, in which
We build houses. For all of us to be.

Camera of thought, as if remembering.
Tomorrow's colony naked and faint.
His moon is behind me, changing.

Come true. Behold our solid beams.
Afraid of not being, be not afraid.
Some things are better than dreams.

AFTER ANDIL GOSINE,
PORTRAIT NO. 20 FROM (MADE IN LOVE)

The landlady hears the banging of the bed-head
so she makes sure to peep when we leave
to see if it's a man or a woman this time
because it could be a man
sometimes it is a man
a man from some obscure part of the island
like Freeport.

It's always a man.

AFTER RICHARD FUNG, *DAL PURI DIASPORA*

fold. to dream
to tear. of it. a
pageopenspill
beans. neverr-
epeating.recipe
fill. burn home .

.

AFTER JEAN-ULRICK DÉSERT,
AMOUR COLÈRE FOLIE (LOVE ANGER MADNESS)

My mother daily lives in fear of the rain
My mother daily falls and fears like rain
When rain falls we close windows
She watches, she prays, she guards the door.
At nights she plays Buju Banton for us
For we like poetry, and she is worried.
She is worried because of what we spell.
Though we laugh, she hears thunder
Saying: Father, come back.

FATHER'S DAY

Father's Day is coming and all I can think of is Orlando,
not the Virginia Woolf character who changed from a man
into a woman,
or Shakespeare's lover in the Forests of Arden
or Handel's opera sung by an alto castrato,
Orlando, the magic kingdom,
where the gunman mowed us down.

Father's Day is coming and all I can think of is Orlando,
all I can see is Orlando,
all I can breathe is Orlando,
the world is Orlando,
Orlando, Florida's natural,
no longer orange but red.
All those daughters and sons dead.
What are we doing for Daddy?
my sister Whatsapps frantically
What are we doing?
Orlando Orlando Orlando –

CATULLUS IN LIBYA

At nights I removed my penis
but in the morning it grew whole again.
We sat at the shore, the sea's sulcus, & edged
into the light that burns the Sahara. These women
I love make me also love their men; full of semen is my
purse, which pays the price and is paid in return.
I use them as if I had bought them for myself,
again and again their groins bursting
my anus
a flower at the farthest end of the desert
that plows through conquerors with petals.
Yet one day Libya I must flee, as I fled scorched
India, and deny the light that owns my soft marrow.
I will tell them of my love for her, this woman
of sand. My beheaded penis will not come
back like the sparrow on the cedar tree.
A bad rhyme I will be. Fuck me.

LANGSTON HUGHES IN TRINIDAD –
A CLOSET DRAMA IN FIVE SCENES

dramatis personae

ALAIN LEROY LOCKE: a wealthy groupie
COUNTEE CULLEN: Langston's gay best friend
ROMEO LUPPI: a one-night stand in Italy
SYLVIA CHEN: the token secret lover
A SAILOR: whose eyes he never forgot

I. In which Langston Discovers Rivers

There can be no proof of it, but he would not want this performed,
performer all his life. This drama in which he makes love in Nigeria

to a sailor. Lagos. Where Ogun and Osòun meet. He hides forever.
Inside, him. His strapping sailor does not get a name, though we read

of the dialogue they have before sex. *Won't it hurt you,* the poet asks.
Not unless it's square, his mate replies. *Are you square?*

*Could be. Let's see.** Offstage they touch and all Langston can think
is how they look like branches, these fingers, these bulging veins on

mauby skin. Ogun is the god of water. Osòun, the god of needs.
Hold back the river. Let ink flow, speak of dreams. Everything is

black.

*Langston Hughes recalled this story about gay sex with a sailor decades later while
speaking with a secretary on March 25, 1963. Some doubt this account.

51

II. In Which Countee Cullen Realises He's Just Not That Into Me

In another country, wise men make their heaven
And fools are given maps
But here the brave are made to suffer
For being brave *don't tell don't*
ask All flesh is made to die *he knows*
he read my poem then laughed
All leaves fold, like books
he forgets my name

III. In Which Langston Sends Alain Locke Drunk Texts Then Pretends Nothing Happened

"MAY I COME NOW PLEASE LET ME KNOW TONIGHT BY WIRE."

— *Langston Hughes to Alain Locke, Feb 2, 1924*

"Forgive me for the sudden and unexpected message I sent you. I'm sorry… I had been reading all your letters that day and a sudden desire came over me to come to you then, right then, to stay with you and know you. I need to know you. But I am stupid sometimes."

— *Langston Hughes, letter to Alain Locke, Feb 4, 1924*

A flower blooms slower
Than the eye can see.
People who are in love
Write of love, so his letters tell me.
Never said it. They showed it.
He wanted me. He needed me.
He told himself he was using me.
Paris, Venice, Genoa.
In a sentence, a word can be
Felt as belonging first with one
Word and then another.
I will look out for him
In the mirror.

IV. Romeo

The problem was neither man was
as hot as Romeo, the Italian waiter.
Yes, Romeo. Nobody could
compete with a name like that. Or how
he balanced his tray
like he balances lovers; or
the way he showed the way through lush hills
to the sun.
Each leaf was a word Langston never said,
the trees his unwritten rhymes.

V. Do Nothing Till You Hear From Me

Langston Hughes has a secret Chinese lover.
Langston Hughes is not black, he is Native American.
And black.
Langston Hughes' Chinese lover is not from China, but Trinidad.
Nobody in Trinidad is from Trinidad.
Langston Hughes does not meet Sylvia Chen in Trinidad, they meet
in Moscow.
Langston Hughes wrote love poems to Anne Marie Coussey, who
was also from Trinidad.
Sylvia Chen's name is not Sylvia Chen.
Sylvia Chen is not Chinese. She is mixed-race, like Langston Hughes.
No one knows for sure when Langston Hughes was born.
His name is really James.

WALT WHITMAN IN TRINIDAD I

i. On His Novel Against Drinking

Amid the rows of books that run like
lines in this poem, a letter to yourself.
A novel in which you are buried –
your most dangerous part. Walt, all these
leaves won't hide your heart. They won't
stop the grass that will come when the war
brings you to the edge.
       Grass, coming fast. I worship
the moss that grows between the pages
of a book thrown away, until all that
was written is as black as truth,
a fiction, at last, that never lies.

It was your father who used to drink,
who taught you pleasure was wrong.
No song in this song, only ink.
Gold pen your door,
gold men that make you see.
You enter the man your father could not be.
Long-Island Star
Long Islander
Eagle
In your book you write,
Loved reader,
let your children read it.
That our children be yours.
That you become our father,
the father you assume.

ii. Erasure from Page One of Walt Whitman's Introduction to His Novel Against Drinking

THE story   reader

                        moral
                                                        heart
            pages

                                live

                        young man

iii: Erasure from Page Two of Walt Whitman's Novel Against Drinking

Reader, I was that youth

WALT WHITMAN IN TRINIDAD II

Your brother, too, drinks.
You flee to Trinidad.
Our bones as good as yours,
Walking along the walls of Lapeyrouse
Our slavery the same slavery, to music
The rhythm of the Atlantic, true poet of slaves.
The Atlantic, that makes countries passable, translating
The untranslatable. What kind of Carnival band is this?
You shake your cane like a Fancy Sailor,
Chipping away at the asphalt.
It cannot support the weight of your volumes.
I am with you.
You stop for pholourie and doubles, sip water
From a coconut, kneel to tie a man's shoes,
Glitter in your silver hair.
What kind of song is this? –
Canboulay sticks hitting steel pan
Notes dressed as poui trees.
Stop this day and night with me.
But your brother, he returns
In these crowds, his face like
A cowl on each jewelled reveller
Who knows what they are yet not what
They will be. Bones beneath the streets.
The road to Balandra curves.
At last, the cold breeze, the moon,
The sea. On Ash Wednesday, our
Poem folds. We no longer read.
Your first book was your last.

A TRINIDADIAN MAN GOES TO BELFAST AND SEES
THE MOUNTAIN THAT INSPIRED JONATHAN SWIFT

the man sleeping
on the mountain
his giant head on my pillow
all the sparrows have flown from him
and pierced me
swiftly tied
by his eyes
bluer now than
in the club
his cool fingers are white chalk
drawing my face
drawn along cobbled streets
inside a city wall
never again
will I dance alone

CHACACHACARE

The coast draws itself, wave
after wave sketching this study: a broken pier to nowhere,
houses torn down by time,
island in the shadow of island.

Someone has written on a fallen
beam, "JONAH WAS HERE".
No fence is needed.
The trees are poisonous,
they keep the dead.

Butterflies guard what they have hoarded:
beer bottles, porcelain mugs, a microscope.
Everything ends up here,
in the hot mouth of a panting dog.

LAKE

AFTER LEASHO JOHNSON, *LOST AT SEA II*

Freddie loved Jacob but Jacob liked Jackson who said he wasn't that way though in the locker-room he was always hard and everybody thought it suspicious but he would boast about some girl he was dating and cover up the fact that he liked to think about Jacob sometimes when he was alone and he was really into the fact that Jacob was gay and liked him and all that but he felt guilty because everybody knew about it and when Kiwan disappeared from school and not even his mother could find him the first thing Jackson thought was it was wrong for someone to be hurt just because they swam in another direction and besides don't we all love the same water?

THE TAMARIND TREE

We watched it spring up one year, so slender, growing in the box of dirt Dad had made with clay bricks at the front of the house, the type of clay bricks that were sharp and strong on the outside but hollow on the inside and would flake and crumble into powdery red shards when shattered. We watched it, growing behind the mossy grey wall that kept the hillside from coming down on us, the wall's paint peeling as though it were skin, my skin growing blisters and sores and boils as we played beneath it – the miracle of dirt, the consequence of building cities, marching armies through the veins of a mud metropolis amid worm and snail, until it surpassed all the children, growing as tall as the house; even then its leaves still delicate: a thin head of hair that let in pockmarks of sun, small patterns all over the walls inside our rooms, a barren mass of effulgence that grew as we became adults and our parents children. I, the end of myself, mysterious and finite, like a wall pushed slowly by the powerful hulk roots of a tree, a wall at first made gently swollen, and then beset by cracks, fractures that grimace under the strain, until the concrete has lost the battle and is made inconsequential. We let the tree continue to get even thicker, respiring at nights above the house, as the roof, now in its shadow, looked on with longing, the house slowly cut open like an eternal wound, buried daily by mounds of fine tamarind leaves, each a written notice, warning of the coming rains and our eviction.

THE FORGETFUL FRIEND

She forgot the days they made love, though this was an important detail for him. Though she did not forget birthdays, she forgot mutual trips to the cinema, fetes and romantic dinners out. He was worried she was erasing him and would not know who he was when she got older. She said it was okay because she had ADHD and it was common for people to forget things. She was getting electro-pulse therapy to the head to improve her memory. A childhood trauma had caused bad signals. She forgot his name sometimes, and he would get angry. He implanted memories, but she erased them with furniture. She liked to buy wooden stools and their apartment became cluttered. She eventually forgot she loved him. That was when she started to remember everything else: the fetes, the dinners. She would wake at night wondering about that man she ate mango sorbet with in the Botanical Gardens, but then her *Facebook* page would tell her there was no such man and that she really loved somebody else.

NOT ALL OF CAZABON'S PAINTINGS
HAVE BEEN FOUND

He left clues in the paintings. The longer you look at them the odder they seem. That single cloud casting a shadow on the mountain was the reason for everything. It is no coincidence the trees are bigger than the cathedrals. It was important that the people floated on the pitch lake, dressed in white and carrying parasols. He wanted to capture the terrible space which only bamboo can make.

THE LOST EARRINGS

They fell one night after the movies. Gold in the darkness. We looked everywhere: under the sofa, the settee, the poof. Check beneath the Christmas tree, mother said. There were still a few presents and some wrapping paper that had not been thrown away. The tree had a large red doily in which all kinds of glittering things were lost. The inside of the tree was another tree and another moment in time. This was the second time gold earrings had vanished. The first time was years before when a diamond-studded dragonfly disappeared beneath the stove. She thought she heard the two desktop speakers make the sound of the ocean rumbling. Two people were moaning every now and again, but the audio was on mute.

INSTRUCTIONS FOR THE READING

I talk to myself. So what? Nothing's wrong with that. I talk to myself all the time. I am talking to someone else in their mind. They are responding. Someone is overhearing this conversation. We are all in the same mind. The voices think of talking. The voices think. They talk of thinking. We write. You are what I thought.

They use it to communicate. Some of the poems are by invented authors. They contain codes. The ciphers are scattered in a series of diaries. One particular poet's address changed too frequently. The leader of the scheme is not a poetry editor, but a seemingly occasional critic who turns up at press events every now and then.

YES

They left messages for each other in the visitor logs of art galleries. They were careful. They were never in the same room together. Each day was another day. Each place had a designated function. In the logs, simple instructions were left. They signed using fake names. Their comments sometimes puzzled the art world. Until all the galleries on the island fell. And then they had reason.

THE BEACH HOUSE

When they were much older, our parents ran away from us. The warning signs had been there for weeks. But we did not notice, until they had already escaped. The first clue was how items of food disappeared from the kitchen. They were secretly hoarding. Then Dad came home from work one day very early and said he did not have to go to work anymore. Then Mommy – who by this stage was always forgetful of our names – started to work, but we were never sure what she was doing. They would both go for long drives in the country and sometimes come back late at night with plastic bags filled with fruit. The last time we saw them, they said they were going to the beach-house at Redhead Bay in Cumana. When we eventually got there, days later, the beach-house was a shell of nothing but concrete debris and rust. There was no roof, the walls had fallen down years ago and had been overtaken by vines. The bush in the yard was high. No-one had stayed there for ages. One neighbour on the track said she heard things but never looked. The oil-rig glowed in the distance over the sea, a giant orange eye.

THE THIRD PAIR

He found the first pair of spectacles at the bottom of the laundry basket. It was gold. It might have belonged to the old woman who came to the house. People often forgot things in the birdcage. The second pair was in the back-seat of the car. Rimless, but in a gold case, it made itself into a knife. The man buried the woman in sand at Maracas. When he went into the water, she could not move.

THE HANDSHAKE

No poem is enough for you. Your eyes still new, even after ten years. The eyes that first opened. From across the room, every day. A year. Your eyes ten years. Your voice a rock. Your body an island hiding off the coast. Your confusion, confusing. Your teeth as hard as chaos, as loud as water. You come with sun, and leave with it. No time for talking. You borrow pens. You touch my hand. You take my book. You take my poems. You are the inside of you. Misinformed, do not hide. Disappointment. The time is not right. Exhale, you cannot. You panic to be found, naked. Your eyes are sweet nipples. You are a razor against my skin. You promise the sea. Seal my mouth, your hair is long, then you cut it short. Never say goodbye. You wear a black veil. You throw sand in my eyes. You wave. You surround. You won't let go of my hand. After ten years, a handshake.

AT THE GYM

She was such a sweet girl. He pumped her full of steroids. Her hair became translucent. She wanted to match his biceps. People said she was such a sweet girl before he turned her. Eyes as muscular as a wrestler's, she became adamantine. She developed a powerful regime, and exceeded all of his male friends at the gym. He had many. She liked it. When he asked for further adjustments to her breasts — a reduction — she eagerly agreed for the change would help her lift dumbbells. She was such a sweet girl, he ate her. One day he saw blood on the gym floor and screamed.

THE CRYING LIGHT

That the light behind my Blackberry had gone on had escaped me. In fact, it had been on all week, glowing like a piece of paper. Because I only looked at the phone's face, I never saw what was going on behind it. Until one day a cement truck turned down Chacon Street from Queen Street and pulled down all the electricity lines. The office was plunged into darkness; we had no windows through which natural light could come in. I got lost in the dark. But there was this light, already shining for me, showing me the way out. From the back of the theatre, the owner of the cinema supervised our pleasures. He wanted to convince us that he should be allowed to build an island off the coast and on it house a street for every city of the world. We were deep into it without realizing.

THE CLOCK-TOWER
IN FRANCIS FORD COPPOLA'S FILM *TWIXT*

The clock-tower has five faces, each with the same model of clock: white and with black letters in an old font. Each clock tells a different time. These are not the different times of different time zones, but different times pure and simple. When you look at the tower, you have no idea what time it is, what day it is. Each clock is like a one-word poem that seems to last forever.

A PRISONER had escaped and the news made everyone nervous. The townsfolk were not unused to crime. Robberies and murders had happened over the years; there were whispers of gangs and drug blocks, and the sprawling suburb that rose into the verdant hills of the Northern Range had – unjustly, the locals would insist – developed a reputation in the media as a crime hotspot. But the idea that The Muslim had got a hold of a gun, shot his way out of the Port of Spain jail and fled to Belmont was trouble of a new kind.

Nobody learned of these developments faster than Mrs Holder. She immediately took the precaution of double-locking the sheds in her garden and, for the first time in the decades since her husband died, reconsidered her habit of walking alone to mass. That Friday afternoon there was heavy rain again. The skies were dark. It was dreary and dim. The police were everywhere. One patrol managed to fit into the narrow lane where Mrs Holder lived, its siren silent but its blue lights flashing, bouncing off the lace fretwork of the houses.

Mr Samlal, Mrs Holder's tenant, was still at The College where he taught art. He gave extra lessons and would normally be home after six. She looked out for him.

"All this police now for what?" Mrs Holder said when Mr Samlal came out of his car. "I don't blame that man for getting out yes. Those macomères does do all kinds of things to man inside there." Mr Samlal struggled with his umbrella, trying to balance it with a large blank canvas he was carrying. He had moved in soon after he took up his teaching job, fresh out of university, five years ago.

"Trinidad too corrupt yes," Mr Samlal said. "Somebody had to help him with that gun. I sure people see things and just too coward to tell the police."

"Well I tell you what, I ain't see nothing, I ain't hear nothing, I ain't know nothing," his landlady said. "Percy say he coming tomorrow please God. I told him we need another man around the place." Mrs Holder's husband was dead but, as she often pointed out, she was not. She had met Percy a few months ago during Carnival while she was playing mas, which she managed to do devoutly every year.

The house was a series of interlocking apartments. Like many families in the lane, Mrs Holder had, over the years, expanded her home and rented out the extra rooms. There were three tenants in all, but weeks could pass without them seeing each other.

Safe inside his apartment, Mr Samlal put down the blank canvas. He lived alone. He had set up one room as a studio, where he would store his art supplies and paint late into the night. There was not much furniture in the apartment. Colourful paintings leaned against the walls. He did not hang them because he was not sure where each should be placed and did not want to risk making a permanent mistake. So while he had been living in the lane for almost five years, the apartment had the feel that someone had only just moved in. There was no television set. But he had seen the broadcasts about the jailbreak in the staff-room at The College, the picture of The Muslim plastered all over the screen, with police warning the escapee was armed and dangerous. Mr Samlal had a thought. He decided to go into each room and turn on the light, doing a quick search of the closets, under the bed, in the bathroom. He even looked inside his fridge, which in his estimation was large enough to hold a fugitive. Assured that he was alone, he locked his door and closed the burglar-proof gate.

After his evening exercises and meditation, Mr Samlal had dinner and stared at the blank canvas. It was for a new student who would begin lessons tomorrow. The initial plan had been for the student to come to Belmont for his first class. But that changed after Mrs Mendonca rang Mr Samlal at school earlier in the afternoon, saying she had no prejudice against Belmont and its people but would rather that her son's lessons not take place there in light of recent developments. Could Mr Samlal simply come to their house in Cascade?

Mr Samlal agreed. Cascade was only a ten-minute drive from Belmont. But to Trinidadians, the difference between the two neighbourhoods was an entire world. He thought about this as he settled into bed. After he fell asleep, more rain came, splattering on the windows. The night was chilly. Not far from where he slept, Mrs Holder made one last inspection of her sheds, carrying an umbrella and torchlight into the garden before she, too, went to sleep.

JEAN-PAUL was a bright student but his grades never matched his promise. He liked Geography, was competent at Mathematics and enjoyed Literature. But his scores in recent months were falling. He first came to Mr Samlal's attention as part of the group that would hang out every day after school in the art room at The College, waiting for their parents. Mr Samlal liked to run his art room in a democratic fashion. He allowed students of all kinds to stay, to mix with the art students even if they did not study art themselves. He encouraged conversation, particularly on topics revolving around world events or life lessons he felt every boy should learn. Jean-Paul was small in stature, but still managed to stand out for a boy of 15 because he was articulate and frequently challenged Mr Samlal. This was what first drew the teacher to him. But one day his curiosity deepened when the child did something else.

When no one was around, Jean-Paul showed Mr Samlal a small sketchbook. There were paintings and drawings, would Mr Samlal look at them? The child's style was unpolished, he did not have a fine attention to detail. But his forms and his colour palette – which appeared to be intuitively worked out – were striking. There was something about these first images: strange, psychedelic terrains, human bodies and angels rendered with raw feeling, without orna-mentation, as though they were windows to his soul.

Mr Samlal encouraged Jean-Paul to paint and draw more. Finally, he suggested the student take up art as an extra subject; he would provide free lessons. The child's mother was pleased with the idea that her son had been singled out in this way. She agreed to let Jean-Paul attend art class on the weekends.

The Mendoncas' house overlooked a cliff in a part of Cascade where the homes competed with thick forest. The road there was long, narrow and dangerous. It had been dug up by WASA after a water-main burst. The car avoided several orange cones and signs saying "Men at Work", though where these men were working was not immediately apparent. A teak fence and a gate sealed the structure from the road, but once through, the house unfolded like a piece of origami. The family – which had connections with the School Board and the Old Boys' Club that ran The College – was wealthy. The house was modern, built of concrete, wood and glass. There was a swimming pool to the back, done as an infinity pool overlooking steep hillside.

Mrs Mendonca was a lawyer and her husband was in banking. The two had married recently. She was not Jean-Paul's mother, but his stepmother. His mother had divorced Mr Mendonca years ago.

"Thanks so much for this," Mrs Mendonca said. "I'm really pleased you were able to come up. I would have had no problem dropping Jean-Paul in Belmont, but with the escapee on the loose I didn't feel comfortable. Maybe when things settle back down. How is it over there for you?"

"Is normal," Mr Samlal said.

"I don't know how I would be able to live in a place like that," Mrs Mendonca said. "Jean-Paul, Mr Samlal reach! I'll leave you two here, I have to go out for a few things."

A space was set up in the dining room for the lesson. Mr Samlal had walked with the blank canvas. He wanted to get his new student to experiment with a larger scale, see what the results would be. Jean-Paul wore jeans and a T-shirt shirt.

"It weird having my teacher in the house," Jean-Paul said. Mr Samlal asked him to paint something, anything he wanted, on the canvas. He told him how to prepare the brushes, gave him acrylic paints to use (which he had brought over from his own studio), and suggested that he do a light sketch first. He wanted to see how the formal structure of a canvas – instead of a small sketchbook – might affect the child's processes.

There was no difference. The boy painted something abstract, with loose brush-strokes, united by the same palette seen in his smaller pieces. It was as though his painting came straight out of his DNA. Mr Samlal did little talking. He watched.

"What do you think of ISIS?" Jean-Paul asked.

"ISIS?" Mr Samlal said.

"We can't get rid of them if Assad stays in power in Syria," the boy said. "And Putin is doing more harm than good."

"Well, I am glad to have your assessment of the situation," Mr Samlal said. "What are you painting?"

"I don't know; it just came to me," the student said.

"How long have you been doing these paintings?" Mr Samlal said.

"It may have started about three years ago, after they separated."

"What's he painting?" A man, wearing only crumpled white boxers, came into the room. His hair was dishevelled, as though he had just awoken. The flesh of his hairy chest was reddish, with the kind of bruise-like marks left when someone has slept for a long time in the same position. Jean-Paul dropped his brush.

"Mr Mendonca, sorry if we disturbed you," Mr Samlal said. "We were just wrapping up."

Mr Mendonca came over to Jean-Paul and playfully tackled him, locking his neck in one arm, while ruffling the child's hair with his hand. Jean-Paul seemed uncomfortable.

"It reminds me of *The Scream*," the father said, looking at the son's painting. "Well you fellas, don't mind me, I not an expert."

"I've just been asking Jean-Paul how long he's been doing these paintings," Mr Samlal said. Mr Mendonca answered for the child.

"Must have been recently," the father said. "Then again, God knows what the hell he does be doing in that room all day. I tired tell him he need to go outside more. Speaking of which, you clean the yard yet?"

"No," Jean-Paul said.

"Why don't you leave these paints and go do that," Mr Mendonca said. "Remember you have swimming class today, too. Where your mother?"

The child did not answer as he left the room.

"I think Jean-Paul will do well as an artist," Mr Samlal said.

"Listen, don't fill his head with stupidness. Right?" Mr Mendonca said. "This is just a hobby. He can't make any money from it and to be frank I don't like the idea of him getting involve in all that fassy stuff."

He watched carefully as Mr Samlal packed everything and then walked him out of the house, past the serenity pool in the front which was filled with koi that looked like underwater flames.

Something about the painting, Mr Samlal thought, as he drove back down the long, rough road to Belmont.

*

THE PETIT CARÊME came days later. The short spell of dry weather was early. It was a break from the daily thundershowers: bright, hot weather making everything momentarily clear. For the next class, Mr Samlal thought he should take Jean-Paul on an outing before the days of brilliant sunshine ended and the rainy season returned.

The first stop was the National Museum which, five decades after Independence, still bore the formal name of The Royal Victoria Institute. There were some watercolours by Cazabon in a special room, but these were faded and barely made an impression on the boy. He seemed more drawn to the large paintings of Leroy Clarke. Mr Samlal remarked on the colours, the artist's use of every inch of the canvas, the intricate attention to detail, the richness, the suggestion of narrative, myth, folklore. It was a while before he realised that Jean-Paul had drifted away.

Mr Samlal found him in one of the special exhibits featuring the butterflies of Trinidad. Jean-Paul stared at the yellows, blues and greens of the creatures, their etherised rows flying to some unknown destination. The art teacher used the opportunity to give Jean-Paul a drawing exercise: he asked him to do a quick sketch of his favourite butterfly.

The next exercise, however, would be more trying.

Mr Samlal took him to Macqueripe Bay. He hoped the change of scenery would invigorate his student, make him relax and open his eyes to art in nature and the world around him. He asked him to make sketches of the children playing ball on the shore, their bodies dark against the glittering surface of the water. It was one of those rare moments in education where pleasure met professional obligations: Mr Samlal planned to take a quick dip to cool off from all the heat while Jean-Paul was sketching. In the car-park, he changed into trunks. After he finished swimming, he made his way to the showers outside the changing rooms and washed himself. It was a while before he realised Jean-Paul was watching him from the car. When their eyes made contact, the child quickly averted his gaze. Of course, Mr Samlal thought, the boy might be gay. That is what his father senses. That is why he is so aggressive.

"Do you do your own paintings?" Jean-Paul asked on the drive back. Mr Samlal smiled, deciding there would be a third stop.

The studio in Mr Samlal's apartment looked as he had left it. Paints were all over. His latest canvases were scattered on the floor. He liked to work on more than one piece at a time.

It was getting late. The sun was going down. Jean-Paul asked Mr Samlal about a particular piece at the far end of the room. They stood before the canvas. Blue, grey, gold: a city scene, a church, some people, a vendor. The student placed his hand over his teacher's hand. Mr Samlal withdrew immediately.

"I should take you home," he said.

In the car, there was silence as they drove through the streets of Belmont, passing the road where the police station was, blue cars parked outside as though waiting expectantly.

"My parents won't like to hear that you took me to Belmont," Jean-Paul said. "The Muslim is still on the loose."

"It's fine, there's nothing to be afraid of," Mr Samlal said, irritated. "Despite what people say, the area is very safe and—" Before he could finish the car made a strange noise and stalled.

Mr Samlal got out and took a look at the engine. He was not good with cars. It was now dark. The street was quiet. A small group of men were liming on the corner. When the group noticed the car had stalled they began to approach. Mr Samlal slammed the bonnet shut.

"What's the problem, Father?" one of the men, wearing a wife-beater and red trousers asked.

"I think it's the battery," Mr Samlal said, as all the men surrounded him. He looked at Jean-Paul sitting in the car.

"Small thing, we go help you push," the man in red said. Mr Samlal tried the ignition one last time. It started. He thanked the men and sped away, taking Jean-Paul to Cascade.

When Mr Samlal got back to Belmont, Mrs Holder was waiting in her veranda. He told her what had happened with the car, though he didn't mention that he had a passenger.

"Is only good people living Belmont," Mrs Holder said. "Is foreigners coming here who giving we a bad name."

*

THE ART lessons stopped. Mr Samlal cancelled the next session saying he was ill. He did not know how to handle the situation. He was mindful of the Mendoncas' connections and did not want to cause upset in any way.

The boy stopped coming to school for a few days, which was not unusual for him; other teachers reported him as frequently absent. But given who he was there were never any serious repercussions. This was a fact of life in The College; some students were special and special accommodations had to be made.

One day, there was a fight in the art room. Jean-Paul was one of the two boys feuding.

"What's going on here?" Mr Samlal asked.

"Nothing," Jean-Paul said as the other boy scampered away and the group of students left.

"Where have you been?" Mr Samlal said.

"We went Tobago," Jean-Paul said.

"Did you take your sketchbook?"

"I didn't," Jean-Paul said. "We didn't have time for stuff like that."

Mr Samlal noticed a red mark on the boy's arm, a bruise.

"Why were you fighting?"

"It was nothing," Jean-Paul said. "Leave me alone!" His loud tone startled Mr Samlal, who felt self-conscious. He watched the boy storm off.

That night, despite his evening exercises and meditation, Mr Samlal's mind was a mess. He didn't like how things had turned out. And now he was worried about the possibility that Jean-Paul might be the victim of a school bully. He decided he would continue the art lessons that week and he would also approach the Mendoncas on the possibility that the child was being harmed.

On Saturday, he returned to the house at Cascade. Though he had made arrangements with Mrs Mendonca, when he knocked on the large red gate there was no response. Mr Samlal rang the house phone, but no one answered. As he was about to leave, he heard something. An animal, a scream.

"Jean-Paul!" Mr Samlal cried out. He heard the gate unlatch. Mr Mendonca came out.

"Mr Samlal, how long you out here?" Mr Mendonca said, as though he already knew the answer.

"Not long," Mr Samlal said.

"Sorry, but my wife and Jean-Paul not here," Mr Mendonca said.

"She said she called you. But you can still come in if you like." Mr Samlal jumped at this chance. He walked into the living room.

Jean-Paul was inside, sitting on a sofa.

"I thought he wasn't home," Mr Samlal said.

"Yes, I thought you weren't home, Jean-Paul," Mr Mendonca said.

The child was breathing heavily.

"I don't think it's a good day for lessons, Mr Samlal; we'll see you next week," Mr Mendonca said.

On the drive back down, Mr Samlal thought the whole thing was strange. He went over the visit. After Mr Mendonca spoke he had raised the issue of the fight at school that week, and – in the child's presence – suggested to Mr Mendonca that there might be a bully targeting him. Mr Mendonca listened intently. He did not take his eyes off his son. When Jean-Paul eventually left the room, Mr Samlal got a glimpse of a bruise on the child's arm. Was it the same bruise? Was it the same arm?

Then he realised Jean-Paul did not have a gay crush on him as he had thought. The paintings which he painted were not just expressions of teenage angst, they were signs of trauma. The child had shown them to him as a cry for help. His father was abusing him.

Mr Samlal stopped the car and parked by the Savannah. It was late afternoon, there were joggers and people selling coconuts. A rugby team practised near The Hollows, families picnicked and newly-married couples posed for photographs in the nearby Botanical Gardens. From where he parked, Mr Samlal could drive off the main road and onto the street that led to the Belmont Police Station. Or he could continue along the roundabout and head straight home. His moment of revelation, the sudden clarity of it was like a shock. He had to report this to the police.

But what did he really know? No, he thought, he could prove nothing, did not know for sure. Who would believe him? His word against Mr Mendonca, the powerful, wealthy man from Cascade, with ties to the School Board and the Old Boy's Club. No, he thought, trying to convince himself, I don't know anything at all. He took the route that led away from the police station, driving fast.

That day Mr Samlal looked forward to speaking with Mrs Holder when he got home.

"Mrs Holder, they find The Muslim yet?" he said.

Where Mrs Holder would normally be, a man was in the veranda, sitting quietly. He held a cigarette in one hand and a mobile-phone in the other.

"Am sorry I didn't see you there. Have you seen Mrs Holder?" Mr Samlal said. The man said nothing in response.

Mr Samlal recognised the man's face, but could not recall from where. He could have sworn he had known this person for years. Or was this the feeling of déjà vu you get when you are very tired? The man got up from the chair and approached him.

That night, the rains returned. Mrs Holder made sure to carefully lock her garden sheds.

MISTAKEN IDENTITY

I thought it was him and could not stop staring. When he came forward I smiled. He smiled back. Afterwards, I realised it was the wrong person. But when next he saw me, he remembered our last encounter and so smiled again and came forward again. I smiled back. For years now we've been friends.

JOURNEY BY NIGHT

We were walking down the street and suddenly we could not pass. A huge band of people, complete with music trucks, blocked the road. The security men put ropes on the street and stopped people from passing. It was a public road and suddenly, there was no freedom. Dancing and music.

LIGHTNING

Mother was gone so the house felt bigger, the rooms felt bigger, we could dance, we could run, the three of us could play before she came back with her big brown bag of market stuff, smelling like Charlotte Street. She was gone and suddenly everything was sweet: the staircase became dangerous, the walls epic barricades protecting us from the invading forces beyond the guava tree. When the thunder began, Shirley started to howl and my sisters said I should go and untie her. But I looked outside and the world was in darkness, and although I felt sorry for Shirley – who had miscarried a few weeks prior after a difficult pregnancy – my fear was greater than my compassion. But she kept yelping, making a terrible howling noise that I had never heard her make before, even when she had given birth to the dead pups. So I put on my blue rubber slippers and went to the galvanise kennel Father had made for her. My sisters said that after they found me they had to call Tantie who then drove to meet Mommy who came back home in a panic because they said I had been struck by lightning, though later, under their warm blankets as I lay flat on the living room floor, I quietly read what happens when you are struck by lightning and doubted I could have survived such a process. Since then, I've been wondering whether I really survived, whether all this is a dream, stretching into years – all while I am still in that wet kennel hugging my dog because I don't want her to die.

PITCH LAKE

Black.

ACKNOWLEDGEMENTS

Poems were first published or are forthcoming at: *Asian American Literary Review* ('Langston Hughes in Trinidad: A Closet Drama in Five Scenes'); *Afrikana.ng* ('Monday', 'The Undersea Volcano'); *Almost Island* ('Lake Chad', 'Erasure of Horace's Epode IX', 'Shells', 'The Beach House'); *Cordite Poetry Review* ('After Olive Senior, "Flying"'); *Interviewing the Caribbean* ('The Gaol at Port of Spain', 'On Walcott's *Ti Jean and His Brothers*'); *Jai Alai* ('Loros Guaros'); *Likewise Folio* ('The Clocktower in Francis Ford Coppola's Film *Twixt*'); *Moko* ('The Gym', 'The Haircut', 'Kiskadee'); *past simple* ('Kiskadee', 'Redhead Bay, Cumana'); *The Miami Rail* ('After Charl Landvreugd, *Movt nr. 8: The quality of 21*', 'After Jean-Ulrick Désert, *Amour Colère Folie (Love Anger Madness)*'); *The Poetry Review* ('The Forgetful Friend', 'Not All of Cazabon's Paintings Have Been Found', 'Yes', 'The Third Pair'); *The Caribbean Writer* ('On Wordsworth's *The Daffodils*', 'On Titian's *Diana and Actaeon*') and *Visual Verse* ('Love').

My catalogue of unabashed gratitude further includes: D.M. Aderibigbe; Cynthia Birch; Loretta Collins Klobah; Christopher Cozier; Annalee Davis; Joan Dayal; Elron Elahie; Marcus Espinoza; Ann Marie Goodwin; Arden Heerah; Alex Johnson; Nicholas Laughlin; Sean Leonard; Josh Lu; Geoffrey MacLean; Ruth McCarthy; Sharon Millar; Gene Moreno; Martin Mouttet; Wendy Nanan; Shivanee Ramlochan; Monique Roffey; Marina Salandy-Brown; Nicholas Sosa; Hannah Bannister; Jeremy Poynting; Luis Vasquez La Roche; my family.

This book is for Mervyn Taylor, Breanne Mc Ivor and Caroline Mackenzie.

ABOUT THE AUTHOR

Andre Bagoo is a Trinidadian poet and writer. He is the author of *Trick Vessels* and *BURN*, which was longlisted for the 2016 OCM Bocas Prize for Caribbean Literature. His poetry has appeared at journals such as *Almost Island*, *Boston Review*, *Cincinnati Review*, *Caribbean Review of Books*, *St Petersburg Review*, *The Poetry Review* and elsewhere. He was awarded The Charlotte and Isidor Paiewonsky Prize by *The Caribbean Writer* in 2017. *Pitch Lake* is his third book.